If you were me and lived in...
CHINA

A Child's Introduction to Culture Around the World

Carole P. Roman
Illustrated by Kelsea Wierenga

Dedicated to Conny Crisalli, whose friendship
and guidance makes everything perfect.

Special thanks to Johnny, a very helpful and patient waiter.

Dedicated to my mother. - K.W.

Copyright © 2013 Carole P. Roman

All rights reserved.

ISBN-10: 1-947118-83-8

ISBN-13: 978-1-947118-83-6

Library of Congress Control Number: 2012921018

Disclaimer:
Please note that there may be differences in dialect that will vary according to region. Multiple individuals (from each country) were used as sources for the pronunciation key but you should be aware of the possibility of alternative pronunciations.

If you were me and lived in China (Chai-na), your home would be in East Asia (Ay-sha). China is officially known as the People's Republic of China and has 1.35 billion people living there. It is the most populated country in the world.

China has a wide variety of climates from grassland areas called forest steppes (steps) and the Gobi (Go-bee) and Taklamakan (Tak-la-ma) deserts in the dry north to the subtropical forests in the wetter south.

China has two famous rivers. The Yangtze (Yang-zee) is in the south, and the Yellow River is in the north.

The name China comes from the way people tried to pronounce Qin (Ch-een). The Qins were a family or dynasty that ruled China over two thousand years ago.

You might live in the capital Beijing (Bay-jeeng). It is often called Peking (Peek-ing) by people who don't know the correct way to pronounce its name. People have lived in this ancient city for over three thousand years, and it is the political, cultural, and education center of China. It also is a major spot where highways, trains, and expressways meet. The airport is the second busiest in the world. It is famous for all the temples, parks, palaces, and gardens found there. Leaders called emperors (em-per-ors) lived in the Forbidden City, which has a very big and beautiful palace. It has over four thousand rooms with many hidden or secret chambers. Some are so secret, they haven't been discovered yet! They started building the palace in 1406 and finished it in 1420. It took fourteen years!

Parents in China pick names that have meanings, so if you are a boy, they might have chosen An (Ah-n), which means peace. Bao (Ba-ou) is another word for treasure, and Fu (Foo) means happiness.

If you are born a girl, they might have picked Hong (Hom) because they like the color red. Yu (Eeu) stands for Jade, which is a pretty gemstone. Zi (Zzz) is the word for smart. Which name would you want your parents to choose?

Wo ai ni Mama (Woo eye nee Maa-ma) is how you would say, "I love you, Mommy." The word for Daddy is Baba (Ba-ba). Can you say, "I love you, Daddy" in Chinese?

When you go to the store to buy a wawa (wa-wa) for your baby sister, Mama will used renminbi (lem-ming-bee) to pay for it. What do you think a wawa means?

There are so many places to bring visitors when they come to China. For years, people from other countries could not see any of its wonders, because China did not allow people from foreign countries to visit. You most certainly would take them to see the Great Wall of China. It is a long, stone barricade or fence built over thousands of years to keep out strangers from China. No one is sure how long it actually is, but estimates are around fifty-five hundred miles.

You may want to see the giant terracotta (ter-ra-cot-ta) or clay army that was recently discovered buried underground approximately two thousand years ago. It is the most popular tourist spot, and there are over eight thousand individually sculpted soldiers that were made to protect Qin Shi Huang (Cheen-Zzz H-wan-g), the first emperor of China. There are also statues of 520 horses and 130 chariots.

The food you eat would depend on where you live in China. In Beijing, your mom would cook in the Mandarin (Man-dar-in) or northern style. Your favorite meal would be Peking Duck because of the crispy skin and tasty meat wrapped in a pancake. She would make delicious noodles with your meal.

When you visit your cousins in the south, you would enjoy a Cantonese (Can-ton-neese) dinner with stir fried rice with sweet and sour pork. Grandma, who might live in the southwest, would cook in the Szechuan (Szz-u-yaun) style, which would be very spicy and include a lot of chili peppers.

A special treat would be to eat the seafood in the Shanghai (Sh-ang-hai) area found in the southeast of China.

Either way, you would love to finish your meal with fried ice cream! The frozen treat is rolled in breading and quickly stir fried for an amazing experience.

Tea or cha (ch-a) is always enjoyed with your meal.

Of course, while you might enjoy skiing, basketball, soccer, or baseball, your favorite sport would have to be table tennis or ping pong. It is a very popular recreational sport in China. You would love to participate in tournaments and work hard to perhaps even play in the Olympics.

In 1972 when China was closed off to the rest of the world, Ping Pong Diplomacy (Dip-plom-ma-see) brought the many nations together. When the U.S. Table Tennis team was invited to play, it opened the doors for China and the United States of America to have a relationship.

When you see your mother busy sweeping the entire house, and Baba is painting all the windows and doors with a new coat of red paint, you would know that the New Year or Spring Festival is approaching. Mama must put away the broom and dust pan before the holiday starts, so she won't sweep away any of the good luck!

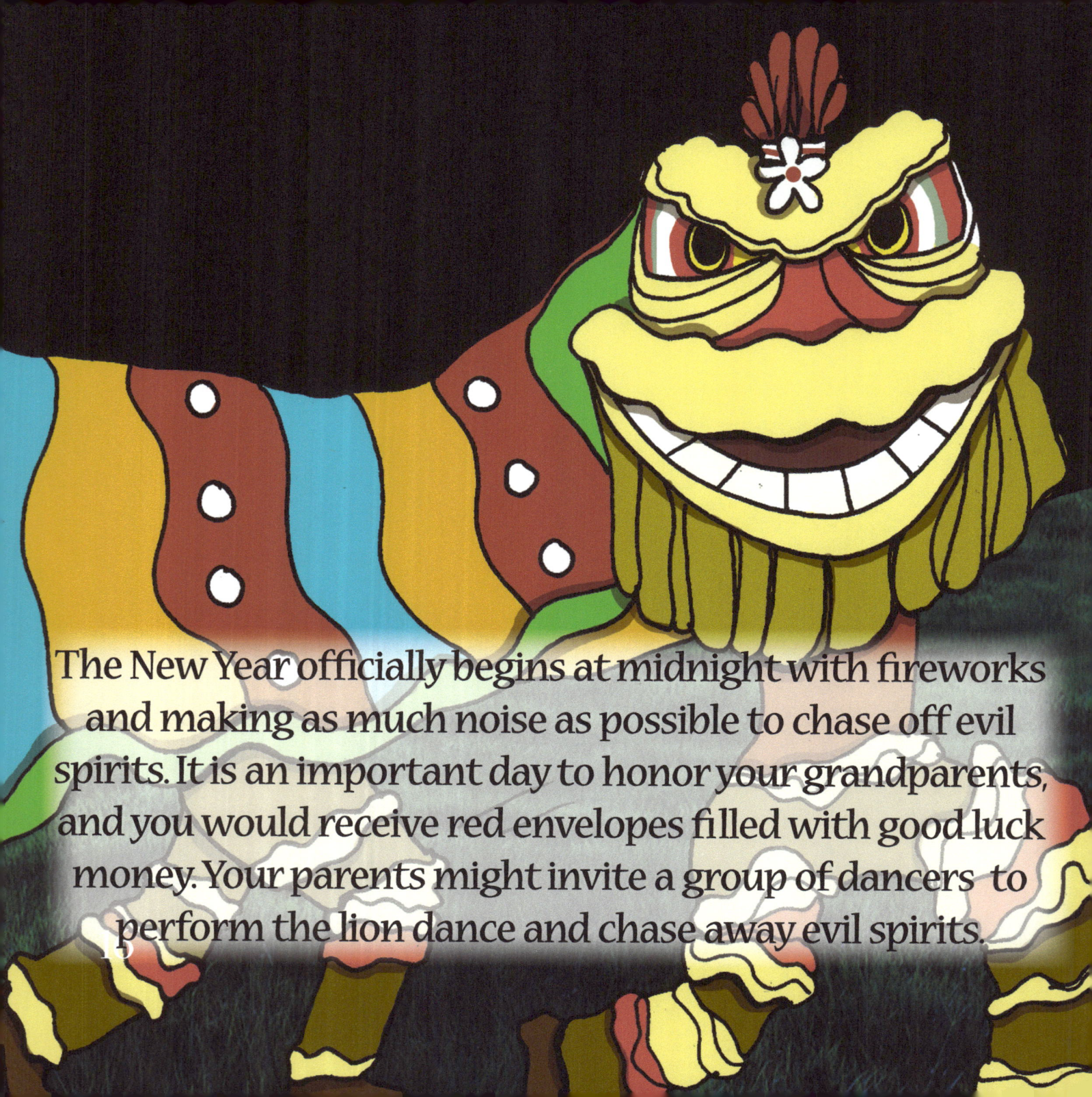

The New Year officially begins at midnight with fireworks and making as much noise as possible to chase off evil spirits. It is an important day to honor your grandparents, and you would receive red envelopes filled with good luck money. Your parents might invite a group of dancers to perform the lion dance and chase away evil spirits.

There will be many delicious meals, because the celebration lasts fifteen days! Make sure you don't drop your chopsticks, because that could bring bad luck for the whole year!

You will tell all your friends about
it in xue xiao (sh-ue-a she-ow).
Can you guess what that is?

So you see, if you were me,
how life in China could really be.

Pronunciation Guide

An (Ah-n)-popular boy's name that means peace.

Baba (Ba-ba)-Daddy.

Bao (Ba-uo)-popular boy's name that means treasure.

Beijing (Bay-jeeng)-capital of China.

Cantonese (Cant-ton-neese)-ethnic group in the south of China.

China (Chai-na)-People's Republic of China-country in East Asia.

diplomacy (dip-plom-ma-see)-the way countries negotiate rules for peace.

East Asia (Ay-sha)-eastern part of Asia where China is located.

emperors (em-per-ors)-kings of China.

Fu (Foo)-popular boy's name that means happiness.

Gobi (Go-bee)-famous desert in northwest China.

Hong (Hom)-popular girl's name that means red, which represents good luck.

Mama (Maa-ma)-Mommy.

Mandarin (Man-dar-in)-ethnic group in the north of China.

Peking (Peek-ing)-the name of the capital of China that Westerners mispronounce.

Qin (Ch-een)-name of family that became the first rulers of China.

Qin Shi Huang (Ch-een Zee H-wan-g)-first king or emperor of China.

renminbi (lem-ming-bee)-money in China.

Shanghai (Sha-ang-hai)-ethnic group in the southeast of China.

steppes (steps)-grassy plains.

Szechuan (Szz-u-yaun)-ethnic group in the southeast of China.

Taklamakan (Tak-lam-ma)-famous desert in Northwest China.

terracotta (ter-ra-cot-ta)-clay.

wawa (wa-wa)-doll.

Wo ai ni Mama (Wo eye nee Maa-ma)-I love you , Mommy.

xue xiao (sh-ue-a she-ow)-school.

Yangtze (Yang-zee)-river in Southern China.

Yu (Eeu)-popular girls' name that means Jade.

Zi (Zzz)-popular girl's name that means smart.

www.ingramcontent.com/pod-product-compliance
Lightning Source LLC
LaVergne TN
LVHW072310090526
838202LV00018B/2258